Trail of Eternity

Alan York

ISBN: 978-81-19654-49-9

First Edition: 2023
Rs. 200/-

Cyberwit.net
HIG 45 Kaushambi Kunj, Kalindipuram
Allahabad - 211011 (U.P.) India
http://www.cyberwit.net
Tel: +(91) 9415091004
E-mail: info@cyberwit.net

Printed at Repro India Limited.

Contents

Big Ben clock

There in the distance,
In the arms of the mists.
With a share of persistence,
This old tower exists.

Wind blowing around
But the arrows don't stop.
They can't pause their round -
From the bottom on top.

The night has blossomed its flower,
All the stars are scattered like grains.
Only darkness grabbed silent tower
As a cloud that swallows the planes.

It doesn't matter for dawn, -
After labor always a gain!
Sun will come for the crown
And prosperity will near us again.

Forest fairy tale

In the dense thickets of the forest,
Another world lives among the trees.
Here you really feel like a florist, -
Watching the branches sway in the breeze.

Discouraged by the woodpecker's noise,
Frightened deer runs to the lawn.
A living spring will help him apoise,
Quench your thirst and keep moving on.

Gallery of centuries-old oaks and firs
Won't leave anyone on earth indifferent.
Where every sound is a delight to the ears -
It's just impossible to be ignorant!

Looking for berries to bring some
The bear came out of hibernation…
Went to inspect the entire plant kingdom,
Otherwise there will be desperation.

Lulling by the gentle rustle of leaves,
Forest fairy tale enchants with greenery.
I stand without closing my eyelids,
Can't find words to describe the scenery.

Land of the samurai

We are ready to face and repel any raid,
For why then did the ancestors pray?
Real samurai should not be afraid -
Faithful katanas will pave us the way!

We will be the first to meet the sunrise
And the first to spend the sunset.
Pursuing our goal despite the demise -
Even earthquakes are no longer a threat.

Everywhere willow branches that totter -
There are so many places to please the eye.
Sakura flowers slowly fall into the water,
Soaring through the air like storks in the sky.

God has blessed us with a wonderful land,
We have been taking care of it for years.
Every time giving who need a hand,
While ourselves being drowned in tears.

A Song for Robin Hood

If they are hunting for your dexterous
And incredibly quick back,
If they want to see you tortured
With an arrow in your neck.

You always have the right decision, -
I mean a truly sound choice!
How not to make your body beaten
With an angry raging foist.

Robbers, outlaws or just peasants -
Robin Hood will love them all!
Even if you are a thug guy
Or completely poor and small.

Here everyone is for each other,
The branches sway with their hats.
Genteel Merry Men of fortune, -
Not a pack of savage rats.

As a guard who waits for strayers,
Strong as steel this massive oak.
"Nothing wrong with robbing someone –
Who stole it all from his own folk."

Knowing everything in the forest
Like the back of their hand, -
"Serving the crown, are you glad? -
Quit it off and join band!"

They live there without sorrow, -
Simply life despite the laws.
Here the dwelling of free spirits
Is just like living water flows.

Thus, everyone who walks around
And those who live beside the wood –
With all speed they run together
To their homeboy Robin Hood!

Andromeda Nebula

There is one odd phenomena,
So close that you can wave "Hey!"
There is the constellation Andromeda -
Keeping company with the Milky Way.

Maybe that galaxy is not lonely?
Having also planets like Mars.
Not pitch-black emptiness only,
With stars even brighter than ours.

Among myriads of nimble comets,
In front of me I noticed a flare.
Ancient messages of the prophets -
What secrets are hidden there?

Maybe somewhere in this cosmic haze,
Dwells a person the same as me?
Who watches my walks in the maze,
Not even trying to stretch me the key.

In frosty embrace

Do not find heat and sun here -
The bora blow, the foehn's gone.
However, it is great - just trust me,
My boat floats like a swan…

Fjords attract me with legends,
The light is so dim and pale.
With my eyes fixed on the heavens,
I ask Andersen to tell me a tale.

The northern lights shine as lightning,
Coloring all the whiteness around.
With the wrath of formidable Viking -
Rain and thunder will wash our ground.

Do not scare either whirlwinds or trolls,
In the cold there is still something warm…
And while Sif takes care of the souls -
Let the rubbish be swept away by the storm.

Train to Auschwitz

The train rushes like a carriage,
In those wagons they carry us.
From my memories only ravage
And bodies all over the grass.

The place where we are going -
I'm sure full of hobbies and toys.
Through bars the moon is so glowing,
What can possibly ruin my joys?

In halls that are soaked in grace,
With family we'll meet the sunset.
Another will tell you about the place,
I have never been to heaven yet.

Here I am starting to see the camp,
Wire everywhere and the hum of dogs.
One by one we are getting a stamp,
No more opportunity to run to the bogs.

Completely without assault or power,
A smiling soldier approached me.
Called to follow him for some shower -
"Let's swim a bit and you'll be free."

Finally we have come to the bath,
They say it's the way to Eden.
Next to me are parents with friends,
Pity our history can't be rewritten.

Ascent

Mountains inspire just by the appearance,
Delighting the eye with incredible views.
Beauty and grandeur are their inherence
And all the heavy worries need to let loose.

Green ridge of fluffy spruce trees…
The path is paved to the very peak.
But alas, we won't get there with ease
Since every climb is so hard and unique.

The mountain wind blows through clothes,
With its currents pushing me to go forward.
Maybe I will conquer - who knows?
Never been to the roof of the world.

Making my way over the bumps to the top,
Past problems seem to be ridiculous.
There is no any intention for a drop -
You can take the above as a stimulus.

Despite the blows of fate

Despite the blows of fate,
Through thorns I go to a dream.
Despite all the pain and hate,
In the dark I'm looking for gleam.

I make an effort just to subsist! -
Foes want to ruin my procession.
Broken on the cobblestone my fist
But they'll never see my suppression!

Many hands drag me into the marsh,
How can I withstand this savage horde?
Every hit is so painful and harsh, -
Not a moment of rest for my sword.

Beyond vast despair and suffering,
Where I've already reached the goal.
There is bliss and happiness hovering
And just nothing to oppress tired soul.

Somehow I still have those few
Who has always stood with me.
Only with such a faithful crew -
I don't give up and bend the knee.

Lullaby

Sleep my little prince, sleep.
Forget the bad and count the sheep.
Outside the window a firefly flies -
Watching you are slowly closing your eyes.

May only good dreams enter your nights:
Deprived of betrayals or vile envy bites.
Gain strength under the rays of the moon -
The evening is no less important than noon.

Everything on earth gets tired with time,
Be it the sun or a torch in the mine.
Later the hero will come for the treasure.
Since even powerful dragons need leisure.

Crack of smoldering coal in the hearth
Warms our house and warms our hearts.
A light stream of smoke drives away trouble,
Let all misfortunes burst like a bubble.

Sleep my little prince, sleep.
What did today tomorrow we'll reap!
A dying candle stretches the veil, -
It's time to end our lullaby tale.

One of many

The moon shone with its rays,
Encouraging my lonely walking.
Dissolves the longing of past days
And I beg her to keep on stalking.

Face almost covered with snow,
Trembling fettered calloused hands.
Overhead I heard the cry of a crow
Like it's trying to ruin my plans.

Cigarette smoke reflected in the light,
Even here there is a kind of beauty.
Very soon I will finish this night -
A good soldier is always on duty!

A stray bullet leaving a trace,
Went through and shot like a duck.
Tomorrow another will come to replace,
Maybe he'll have better luck...

In the rock garden

There's not a sound to be heard,
Only pebbles and moss…
Like the neck of a crane bird
A row of stones stretched out with gloss.

Here is a monk sitting right in the middle, -
Closed his eyes and went into a trance.
He seems to be solving some kind of riddle
In order to calm the rebellious soul in advance.

Somewhere nearby you can notice a stream,
Carefully carrying fallen sakura leaves.
The shining crimson from the sunbeam,
Showers sparks on ancient temples with eaves.

Forgetting about everything on earth
And meditating until the end of time.
Then you can realize what it's worth,
How in harmony achieve your prime.

Saigon confession

My wound is still bleeding,
There is no strength to run.
All that's left is a pleading
But my work is not done.

I came here holy and clean,
Sacrificed all my freedom.
Now dragging a heavy sin -
On the way straight to Eden.

Life slowly passes my eyes,
Tears run down the smoking rifle.
I've never seen a soldier who cries,
Everything I lived - now just a trifle!

Hurrah! I am falling asleep…
Texas sunset burns like a flame.
The poor widow shouts at her sheep
Like an eagle screaming my name.

Dust of Ages

Among rocks there's silence,
Only scared birds can fly.
Ancient castle stands in compliance,
Simultaneously touching the sky.

Its steps are covered in moss,
Grasping vine expended the pall.
All that remains of the former gloss,
Ruthless ages spare nothing at all...

Tilting my head - I looked at the giant -
As a castle stands on the hills.
During the moment I became self-reliant,
The young spirit is filled up with thrills.

Showing off the surviving tower
And posing with all its greatness.
Evil clouds are circling with a glower
But it still kept all the straightness.

I need to learn from the castle -
"Go forward no matter what!".
Just calmly avoiding the hassles -
My wisdom reflects the shot.

Genesis

One day God decided to punish the earth.
There have already been lizards that creeple.
Earthquakes, volcanoes are not in the dearth.
Soon he accidently gave birth to people.
Why he did it? The question comes first…

Soul of Europe

Great Columbus stares from heaven
At this self-willed, little ship.
Highly worries about,
That it would not hit the reef.

Quietly floating with the flow,
But that ship is not alone –
Since wise and gifted people
Settled there along the zone.

With the patience of the Germans,
The blow of fate is not that hard.
When the one who reads the sermons
Is responsible French heart.

Being gallant like the Danes,
They surely know their faithful way.
Gaily swearing to each other
That one day fortune will pay!

Evil destiny harassed friendly nations,
Sending multiple number of wars.
Brave sailors overcame the situations,
Beyond the sea of blood are the shores.

In the meantime, during terrible weather
And not thinking about the fight;
They are still calmly rowing together
With hope for the future of bright.

Exodus

When the crowd throws stones in the back
And consider you as a loser.
Just go on your way, ignore the whole stack -
You can still outplay the abuser.

Step by step you will reach the Olympus
But only without looking at others.
Feels like an angel giving his nimbus,
You'll see who are foes, who are brothers.

Until then no need to be angry.
Just do things you find best,
Those around will tell you frankly -
"This guy is so strong, the guy is so blessed."

Frustration

Why is this shit happening?
Does that mean the end is near for us?
Life has become more challenging
And it's impossible to live in such fuss.

These wars, murders, slaughter…
Our humanity has gone insane!
Good people are already rotten,
There is no one to break the chain.

Once again, repeating the same mistakes,
We have learned nothing from history.
Being merciful is all it takes -
We don't even have to solve this mystery.

Carrying a burden is hard for angel wings.
From above, the lower world seems so flawed.
They better keep playing their strings,
Even though it's hard to believe in God.

Tempting Australia

Far from us, let's say another planet,
They say it's warm and there are shores.
Only hard to get there - you should plan it
Before you cross seductive doors.

But no worries pals - don't let it frown!
The burning sun is heating here so hot.
Bloodthirsty sharks that dance around
And common fish is also getting caught.

If you are worthy of this unusual place,
Not rude to koalas or even a snake.
Then the country will share all its grace,
Giving a treat of yummy Lamington cake.

Autumn day

Sadness mixed with melancholy
Fascinates me in the morning.
Dousing with rain and volley
Creates a fresh fall adorning.

Washing away dust from the roads
And sprinkling drops on the threshold.
Easy flow helps release perennial loads,
Giving our world a completely new mold.

The plants are finally full of life, -
It was hard to survive such a heat…
After so many weeks of strife:
Revived the maples and even wheat.

Everything outside is covered in gold,
Which only makes chilled soul warmer.
Therefore, even despite the dank cold -
You'll never find a more pleasant corner.

The King and his sons

The king is looking for an heir.
He calls his sons, scratching his hair,
Then three golden-haired princes enter;
Looked around and stood right in the center.

"Which of you is truly worthy of the throne? -
After so many years the challenger is still unknown."
The first, most handsome son approached the king:
"Rule the kingdom – it doesn't hard for me to bring…
French troops, barbarians – all enemies are gonna sink!"

After a minute of silence, the second son begins to speak:
"Come on, I'll conquer the whole world within a week, -
Will rob and devastate the lands because I am sick."
The king kept thinking, preparing to make a choice
But suddenly from afar he heard a voice.

It was the third youngest son who asked to say a word.
"To be a good ruler you don't need to rob the world;
Instead, I would rather build huts for those in need,
Would plant the seeds and fed those who cannot feed."

In the throne room everything seemed to freeze around
While the third son came out with the crown.

Parable of the True Treasure

A young student asks his teacher:
"How can I finally become richer?"
The teacher carefully took off his cloak,
Listened to everything and spoke:
"Oh my dear ambitious student,
How I want you to be prudent…
Rich is not the one with bags of money, -
It won't turn your life into a jar of honey.
All the wealth on earth that you can find
Is safely stored inside your mind."

Toad and dragonfly

A toad sits in the thick of the swamps
Catches pesky mosquitoes and chomps.
Suddenly the dragonfly dances in circles:
"Aren't you tired of the quagmire with turtles?
It's better to live where there is no such smell, -
There are so many places where you can dwell."
Having already heard a lot of buzzing in a day;
Nevertheless, the toad found something to say:
"It doesn't matter where exactly you live,
Whether it is picturesque garden or field.
Even the scariest place please the eye:
Some prefer seaweed, some prefer pie.
True beauty lies merely in our perception
And surely this rule contains no exception."

Parable of the Wise Monk

Two students argue which one is stronger,
Both lost patience to wait any longer.
Ultimately, decided to go to the monk -
Let him choose who is destined to flunk.

They broke into the monk despite meditation:
"Oh sensible master, end this confrontation!
Is it not still clear that I am the toughest?
I dye opponents' faces like an artist's canvas."

The monk frowned as he listened to the two,
Got up and began to slowly move his jaw:
"Without kindness, strength loses it's cost…
Until you realized this, alas, both have lost."

Farewell to the Celts

How not to be joyful and kind?
Admiring such beauty around…
Scotland has captured my mind
With the gloss of emerald ground.

You are forever in my heart,
Comfort in any bad weather.
It hurts so much to depart, -
Lastly, I'll stroke the heather.

Swooping over majestic rocks,
The wind blows so hard and hungry.
Precise as a thousand young hawks:
I'm sure there is no better country.

Castle ruins remind us of the past,
About numerous glorious victories.
Well, I'll take some scotch at last, -
Feel a little sad from valedictories.

Under the canopy of autumn foliage

Fluffing its semi-dry leaves,
Awakened the autumn forest.
With its rustling completes
Sweet-sounding bird chorus.

The trails are paved with gold
Like the road straight to a dream.
Despite the wind that is cold
Among the branches wades beam.

I am happy and enjoy life,
Passing by colorful trees.
The atmosphere is simply divine,
A small park imbued with peace.

Here the oak stands awesome,
Protecting a grown young clover.
In a world of pictorial autumn, -
All the blackness is painted over.

****

Sunday morning.
The organ woke the heavens.
Time without words.

****

It's getting dark.
Ibises paint the sky scarlet.
Live sunset.

****

Medals in the chest.
All that remains of my grandfather.
Grimace of fate.

****

The match went out.
Soaked to the skin, I struggle
to start a fire.

****

Torches on the river.
Cormorants catch trout as they did a
thousand years ago.

****

Sinister glow.
Chestnuts and casings in the grass.
No laughter.

****

Tottori Dunes.
A giant hourglass scattered
its contents.

****

Early morning.
Oroshi howls like a wounded.
Not a soul outside.

****

Toro shimmer
on the way to the temple.
Monks hurry to pray.

****

I'm sitting on
the ocean shore enjoying the rain.
Fish with umbrella.

****

A cicada flew
after me half the way. My good
travel companion.

****

Red light district.
Loneliness for two at a
bargain price.

****

Heather blooms.
Royal purple covered the valley.
I'm a bit of a king.

****

Tar sizzles
on the logs. A fire dragon eats
worthless letters.

****

A flock of ants
drags a beetle mummy. Death and life
go hand in hand.

****

The bamboo grove
is blooming. I won't live to see
the next time

****

Ice popcorn bounces
on the windowsill. Nobody seems
happy about this.

****

The starry sky
Is reflected in a pond
forgotten by all.

****

Wire musical staff.
Metropolis music in a ramp
of evening lights.

****

Ashtray with butts.
In a smoke-filled room,
a flower silently dies.

****

Cold autumn wind.
The cricket quieted down on the empty engawa.
Sorrow pierces the heart.

****

The inscription
on the gravestone: "Died from life.
Death respected him."

****

Great turmoil.
The crowd is out for blood.
It's time to fast.

****

Soul chills.
Into the long-burnt hearth the ubiquitous
mice climbed in.

****

Too late for love
and early for death.
A bell in the distance.

****

The dung beetle rolls
his ball looking up at the stars -
our whole life.

****

Tea is getting cold.
Catching the moon with a spoon.
Thoughts drove away sleep.

****

Wind from the mountains.
The ice pipe awakened the living.
I hope the dog is not chilly.

****

The seagulls anxiously
accompany Yamato beyond the horizon,
as if foreseeing grief…

****

Chicory dyed
the abandoned meadow indigo,
- I'm walking through the sky.

****

The wind brings
spider webs, extending the warm days.
I'm picking ripe pumpkins.

****

Tea's brewing.
The cat came for the sausage -
keeper of peace.

****

A deer rubs
its antlers on a tree, -
samurai in kabuto.

****

It was hailing,
as if the sky were torn. The birds
are pecking for nothing.

****

Bare hashi-like branches
catch the reflection of the moon
in the bowl of the lake.

****

An old door
dangles on rusty hinges. I bought
a one-way ticket.

****

A pair of dragonflies
clutched on the blade. End and beginning,
like sun and shadow.

****

The rain is over.
Beads shiver in the cobwebs.
Stale leaves.

****

I put on a mask
and hurried to a nearby izakaya
to sprinkle the weary soul.

****

A growing moon
like a ripe pumpkin. The sky
tumbled over.

****

Motorway noise.
Pigeons pecking crumbs under
the tables near the bakery.

****

Turtles bask
in the sun, as if they knew
it was Sunday.

****

Silent bell scares birds.
A crowd of people wearing headphones
hurry past the blind musician.

****

The snail has
no need to hurry. Consistency is
the key to success.

****

Street musician.
Yellow leaves in an empty case.
Not one soul.

****

An old man walks along the hot sands.
Years don’t count. Behind the barchan there is
an oasis as a reward.

****

Life is an antique shop.
Everything is available
except youth.

****

It got dark.
Owls circle silently in the sky.
Heavenly guardians.

****

I went down
an old well, found a frog.
It’s fun for two.

****

Sakura color
crumbles, echoing time... The wall calendar
is getting thinner.

****

Dawn has broken.
One by one the street lights
are going out.

****

Time to mourn
but from old age I completely forgot,
where to laugh, where to cry.

****

Clearing out the shelf,
I saw a figurine of Yamato.
O former greatness...

****

The moon, like a stork,
landed on the top of Fuji. It feels chilly.
Peace for a thousand ri.

****

So summer is over.
The bonsai is languishing in
the kitchen little by little.

****

I pulled out the net.
Tina and a few jellyfish.
My dinner floated away.

****

Like a morning garden
of chrysanthemums, in the motley
silk of my beloved.

****

The moon is covered
with clouds. O dear fireflies,
please light my way.

****

Storks leave
the nest. No boundaries,
no limits.

****

The wind spins
a prayer drum in the hope
that heaven will hear.

****

Frozen bunches
of rowanberries. Scarlet rosary
beads in the snow.

****

Angels shed
their wings. Wisteria vine
in purple glow.

****

The cat arched its back,
but she is not a camel.
Grace is her essence.

****

In the evening dawn I feed millet
to the wild ducks. A frog splashed into the water,
leaving the heron without supper.

****

The butterfly fell,
Spinning in the last dance.
A lonely tulip bent.

****

It has rained.
Wet snails on fern leaves.
Time stood still.

****

The silk of the kimono is flawless,
but the peacock doesn't know it. Tail fluffed
and all colors faded in comparison.

****

Be patient.
Roast the barley and cook the beans.
The result will reward you.

****

The grasshopper,
hearing the steps, jumped towards the sky.
I remembered my youth.

****

Old pagoda.
Fragile hope for the best.
Tears on the cheeks.

****

A shard of lentil stew
cold soul. Millet and tea, - the sickness
does not grumble about more.

****

Life is like ice
in a glass with shochu. It melts, leaving
an aftertaste of the past.

****

Wet leaves lined the garden table.
I left a bowl of jam for the bees on purpose.
Joy in my heart.

****

Frosty morning.
The whistle of the kettle spooked
the sleepy sparrows.

****

A faithful dog
whimpered and buried himself in the bristles,
sensing the fate of indifference.

****

Old age took its toll.
I'll go get ready. Why stomp around
the grave in vain?

****

Koi fish are circling
in the pond. Like the sun and moon,
complementing each other.

****

The shards
of Christmas toys sprinkled the sky.
My fate is lost among them.

****

In a dense bamboo grove
the koto moans with an emerald sound.
Even the larks fell silent.

****

Iwo Jima,
breathing a sulfuric stench, raised
ships from the bottom

****

Happiness beans
are capricious, -not all of them spout.
Rubbing Hotei is unlikely to help.

****

What is the use of a melon
in which natural sweetness
hasn't manifiestate yet?

****

It's nice to run barefoot
through the dew in the morning. Don't squash
cicadas as a reward for chirping.

****

Dusk fell.
Like a ray of hope, a firefly
lights my path.

****

Stepping across the
creaky bridge, I take my steps gently so as not to
scare away the gray heron.

****

Turtle comb in her hair,
raindrops dripping down on
her porcelain face.

****

There are grains of
white rice on a plate. Everything outside
is covered in snow.

****

Sakura reflection trembles
in the outlines of the lilies. The hand scooped up ice water.
Mind cleared of thoughts.

****

Winter cold doesn't heed
useless prayers. Holding the breath of life
left no chance.

****

Straw burns
like gunpowder, trying in vain
to continue the fiery dance.

****

I remember my childhood looking at snowflakes.
It doesn't matter that the paint has peeled off the toys.
Time has no power over the memory of childhood.

****

Staff and geta -
what else does a pilgrim need?
Light in the distance.

****

Eyelids closed,
not expecting to wake up. The soul is not
the first time to die.

****

Yujo crying,
giving away love in vain.
Can't sleep.

****

I'm not in a hurry to Paradise.
Did not have time to warm up from the threshold.
Maybe they won't get kicked out.

****

www.ingramcontent.com/pod-product-compliance
Lightning Source LLC
Chambersburg PA
CBHW022203160726
48282CB00024B/311
* 9 7 8 8 1 1 9 6 5 4 4 9 9 *